x ngc

D1632699

PARROTS
AS A NEW PET

J WENTWORTH

...est Anglia
...mbridge

CONTENTS

Photos by Thomas Arndt, Dr. Herbert R. Axelrod, Tom Caravaglia, Isabelle Francais, Michael Gilroy, Fred Harris, Dieter Hoppe, P. Leyser, Horst Müller, Elaine Radford, L. Robinson, Harald Schultz, Vince Serbin, Tony Silva, Carol Thiem, T. Tilford, Louise Van der Meid, Vogelpark Walsrode, Dr. Matthew Vriends, and R. Williams.

t.f.h.

**Published by
T.F.H. PUBLICATIONS, INC.
1 T.F.H. Plaza
Neptune, NJ 07753
Made in the USA**

Introduction

There are some 27 orders of birds in the world which, together, make up the class called Aves. Of these, few are more instantly recognizable than the parrots of the order Psittaciformes. Many species are household names as familiar as those of dog breeds. The budgerigar is the world's most popular pet, while species like the cockatiel are almost as well known. The lovebirds and African Grey Parrots, the Amazon parrots, the cockatoos and the macaws—all belong to the group of birds known as parrots. A great number of parrots are highly colorful in their plumage, but not all. Size varies from the diminutive pygmy parrots (genus *Micropsitta*) of New Guinea, which are a mere 10cm (4in), to the huge Hyacinth Macaw (*Anodorhynchus hyacinthinus*) of South America, which is 100cm (40in), ten times larger.

The most obvious feature of a parrot is its beak, with which the larger species can do tremendous damage and can inflict very serious wounds. A Greater Sulfur-crested Cockatoo could take off your finger without exerting any great effort! Another characteristic of parrots is that they can use their feet like hands (the budgies do not) to grasp food and to clamber from one perch to another or up netting, etc. The most famous characteristic of parrots is their ability to mimic sounds, including our own speech. Not all parrots can talk, and the ability is not unique to parrots, as the Indian Hill Mynah can match any parrot and surpass most of them when it comes to speaking. Although a number of these birds can be distinguished by sex, the majority cannot, so obtaining true pairs is never easy in most species.

Parrots have two forward-facing toes and two facing backward; thus they differ from most birds in the way they grasp

A Blue-fronted Amazon, *Amazona aestiva*. Birds of this species are noted for their beautiful coloration as well as their exuberant vocalizations.

a perch. Most people tend to think of these birds as having short tails, but this is only true of certain species. The long-tailed parrots are usually referred to as parakeets, but not the macaws, even though they too have long tails. In all, there are about 330 species of parrots, many of which take readily to being kept as household pets. Others are totally unsuited for close confinement.

Within the text that follows all aspects of keeping these delightful birds will be covered, together with brief details on those species that are usually more readily available. Having decided on which particular type or group of parrots one wishes to keep, the beginner will find that there is another title from T.F.H. Publications that will cover such

information in detail. This book will not cover in detail individual species of groups of parrots that—because of their size, cost, temperament, difficulty in feeding or similar limiting factor or combination of factors—do not provide good candidates for a beginner's *first* parrot. The macaws and cockatoos, lories and lorikeets, and the hanging parrots are examples of birds for which no species-by-species coverage is provided in the section on beginners' parrots.

Nomenclature

All birds are known by two names, one being the common and the other being the scientific. The former usually stems from an obvious feature of the bird, such as the color of the head. The problem is that breeders in another country might consider that the feature of merit is the chest color; the result is that the same bird is known by two or more common, or local, names. This can cause confusion about exactly which bird is being discussed, because the Gold-chested So-and-so may be a different bird to an Australian than it is to someone in the USA. Likewise, common English-language names will not be understood by a breeder in France or Portugal, as they will have their own common names in their language. Useful in overcoming these problems is that a Swedish naturalist, Carolus Linnaeus (1707–78), devised a method, called the binomial system of nomenclature, in which all

While it is less striking—appearance-wise—than other types of parrots, the cockatiel can, nonetheless, make a fine pet. Cockatiels are noted for their gentle dispositions.

plants and animals are given two names which serve to identify them uniquely as species. In this system all animals are divided into groups, called ranks, based on similarities between them. The higher up the system one goes, the more general are the similarities; the lower one goes, the more they resemble each other. It is like a triangle with life itself at the apex and all the individual species along the base line. The basic language used is Latin, which was found acceptable to all nations; thus whether you are English, Portuguese, Russian, or Chinese the scientific names of animals are exactly the same.

The "class" Aves covers all known birds and is divided into 27 "orders," each containing birds that share numerous features; there are the hawks and eagles (Falconiformes), the ducks, geese, and swans (Anseriformes) and so on, including the parrots (Psittaciformes). The orders are divided, again based on similarities, into "families." In parrots there are the lories and lorikeets (Loriidae), the cockatoos (Cacatuidae) and what are termed the true parrots (Psittacidae). In turn, the families are divided into many "genera" (singular, "genus") in which the birds are by now very similar in most aspects. Members of the same genus that form a single interbreeding group are called a "species." They are given a specific (trivial) name, and only when this is used in conjunction with the generic name do they become a recognizable species. The genus *Agapornis* contains nine members that are all clearly lovebirds and, by adding the trivial name, ornithologists know exactly which one is being discussed. Thus, *Agapornis roseicollis* is the Peach-faced Lovebird; *Agapornis taranta* is the Black-winged Lovebird and so on. It is customary to write the generic and the trivial names in italic, but no other rank. The genus always commences with a capital letter and the trivial always starts with a lower-case letter.

Now, it often happens that there are regional variations in what are obviously the same species and if it is considered these "races" differ sufficiently to justify separate status, then they are called "sub-species." They are identified by having a second trivial name, thus forming a trinomial.

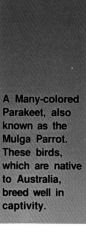

A Many-colored Parakeet, also known as the Mulga Parrot. These birds, which are native to Australia, breed well in captivity.

Stock Selection

The decision to keep a parrot will, depending on the species, need considerably more thought than would normally be required for most other groups of birds. Their powers of destruction are a factor that cannot be ignored—nor can their loud voices. Many are highly expensive to purchase, and most certainly their accommodation could be very costly if the larger birds are the ones that interest you. These factors will influence the ultimate choice of bird, as will the reason why you want parrots in the first place. All parrots can be kept in aviaries, but only certain species are suited to life in a home; some will make better talkers than others.

Purchasing Parrots

Regardless of whether one is buying an inexpensive budgerigar or the most costly of macaws and cockatoos, it should be acquired from a reputable source. Obviously, the more expensive the bird, the more you need to be sure of the seller's honesty. Pet stores, bird farms and breeders are the usual suppliers, but one also sees advertisements from members of the public who, for one reason or another, are selling the more expensive birds. Today, more and more garden centers carry a range of birds and even large department stores have pet departments; finally, many of the tropical bird gardens and zoos also sell off their surplus stock. Each of these sources can be very good or very bad, depending on the standards they keep.

Freshly imported parrots may look somewhat bedraggled but will be fine after their next molt. A first-time parrot owner is better advised to purchase a bird whose condition is superb and which is obviously well acclimatized.

When someone is selling a parrot through their local paper, it might be an excellent buy—but it could just be very bad news, so extreme caution is needed. Maybe the bird has proved to be a very bad pet, the sort that is termed a "bronco" and will not tame. It might be extremely raucous or, in the USA more than in Europe or Australia, it might be a bird smuggled into the country and thus be a distinct health risk.

Further, should problems arise, you have no come-back to the seller, whereas a good pet store or breeder will usually guarantee their stock.

It is possible to purchase a bird via mail order, and thousands of birds are sold in this way. The owners can be very pleased with the service they receive—but the reverse may also be true, and I certainly would

never purchase an expensive bird without seeing it first, unless I was very, very sure of the supplier. When visiting any commercial sellers (pet shops, bird farms, etc.), the general state of

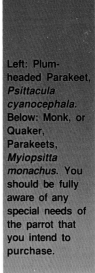

Left: Plum-headed Parakeet, *Psittacula cyanocephala.* Below: Monk, or Quaker, Parakeets, *Myiopsitta monachus.* You should be fully aware of any special needs of the parrot that you intend to purchase.

the place and the cages should be a good guide to the reliability of the establishment. Dirty cages, floors littered with seed and debris, assistants in dirty overalls and the like would make me beat a hasty retreat—assuming I had even entered the premises, which can usually be sized-up from outside. There really is no need to support this type of seller, as there is no shortage of excellent pet shops who have invested large sums of money into ensuring they have first-class cages, equipment and stock, as well as correctly trained and attired staff. A good supplier will not just want to sell you a sound bird, but will want your repeat business of seed, equipment, and maybe more birds. This is the incentive to really ensure you are a satisfied customer.

The Cost Factor

There are two aspects that will need consideration when purchasing parrots: these are the actual cost of the birds and then the price of cages or accommodation. Here we will consider the former.

Price will normally reflect the size, the talking ability or the rarity of the species—or a combination of these. At the low end of the price range will be found budgerigars, cockatiels, lovebirds, selected conures, ringneck parakeets, parrotlets, certain of the small Australian parakeets, and the species like the Senegal Parrot. For those who are interested in breeding parrots, these are ideal birds

with which to gain experience, before attempting to keep the larger and more demanding kinds. Most will make delightful pets, though, other than the budgie and cockatiel, Australian parakeets are not suited to cage confinement. The author, like most people who have kept numerous parrots, can certainly recommend the cockatiel as being one of the most charming and gentle of all parrots, and the lutino varieties are extremely attractive.

Lovebirds, too, can be very amusing birds, but you need to get youngsters straight from the nest to make them really tame. These birds can be quite aggressive towards other birds, and their name is derived from their attachment to their own kind. For many years the ringneck parakeets were so cheap that few breeders ever bothered to breed them, whereas today they are becoming more expensive, especially the mutant color forms, and are delightful aviary birds for the prices asked. They make excellent pets as well. It can thus be seen that you do not have to pay a fortune to have a really enchanting and confiding pet.

Within the next price level are found such birds as the Amazon parrots, certain of the larger Australian parakeets, Mexican parrots, lorikeets and the ever popular cockatoos and African Grey Parrot. To the average pet owner or breeder these birds represent those which they would most like to own. From a breeding viewpoint, many of the rosellas cost no more to keep than a pair of Indian Ringnecks, yet the price that surplus youngsters will fetch will be substantially higher, which is why they are much prized. In addition, they are nearly all very brightly colored.

At the very top of the price scale will be found the giants of the parrot world, the gaudy macaws, the larger of the cockatoos and the rare Australian parakeets such as the Northern Rosella (Brown's) and the king parrots. These birds will be seen in zoos and large private collections, but to most of us their prices are such that, together with their housing needs, they are beyond our pockets in all but a few cases.

The Noise Factor

The idea of owning a parrot such as a Greater Sulfur-crested Cockatoo or a macaw might be very appealing, and tempting if one has the available cash, but it is not as simple as that. These birds have a voice that has to be heard to be believed! It is difficult in words to convey just how ear-splitting a noise they can make—and if it is indoors, in the average-sized room, then your neighbors one block away will be able to hear it. Nor is it restricted to these mighty birds, as I well recall a Mealy Amazon I owned being a source of embarrassment to me when he suddenly decided to exercise his voice. For most of the time he

Another long-time favorite of aviculturists is the Orange-fronted Conure, *Aratinga canicularis*. This bird is also known as the Halfmoon Conure and Petz's Conure.

9

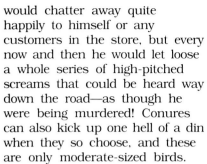

would chatter away quite happily to himself or any customers in the store, but every now and then he would let loose a whole series of high-pitched screams that could be heard way down the road—as though he were being murdered! Conures can also kick up one hell of a din when they so choose, and these are only moderate-sized birds.

So, if you have neighbors, then think very carefully before purchasing a large parrot, and if you plan to breed birds such as conures, Monk Parakeets or the like, then remember that they can be very noisy if a number are kept.

Health

It is obvious that whether you are purchasing a low-priced bird or an expensive one, it should be in very good health. The entire enjoyment of your pet will be made or broken by this fact, so accept no bird that has any sign of being in any other than superb condition. Sometimes a bird that is feather-plucked is offered a little cheaper, and you are told it will soon molt out, after which it will be fine. Take this with a pinch of salt, because once a bird acquires this habit it can be very, very difficult to stop it, and the new feathers are plucked almost as soon as they appear.

Start your inspection of the parrot by taking a general view of it. Does it look lively, do the feathers look neat, are its eyes clear? Does it show interest in you when you approach or does it back off, or growl or hiss at

you?

A healthy bird should have feathers which are held close to its body, its eyes should be round, alive and showing no signs of discharge. The nostrils (above the beak) should be clear of any mucus; if one is larger than the other then it could indicate a recent nasal illness. The upper beak should fit neatly over the lower mandible with no signs of its being damaged. The breast bone should not protrude but should be well fleshed on both sides. The legs should be clean, and all toes should be present (two facing the front and two facing the rear). The vent of the bird should show no signs of heavy staining (caused by diarrhea) or be caked with feces. There should be no unduly loose droppings in the cage.

Judging a freshly imported bird is much more difficult because, as stated earlier, they usually look somewhat bedraggled, with their feathers not in the best of shape. The stress of their journey also makes them look a bit listless at times, as they need time to recover. For this reason these birds are better left to the more experienced fanciers and dealers to purchase, as they are far more able to assess such birds.

Sometimes, even in a really healthy bird, a feather or two might have been disturbed and appear bent or about to come out, and this should not detract from an otherwise obviously healthy parrot. Again, if a bird is actually in the process of shedding its feathers, then it will not look at its best, so either have an experienced fancier with you or select only from birds that are in top condition.

If the bird is to be a pet and it shows excess aggression towards you, I would forget it and look at others. Chances are, it is a few years old and will be far more difficult to tame. A young parrot will, generally, have darker colored eyes than an adult. Another clue are the scales on the feet, which look smaller and smoother in youngsters. The plumage of immature birds may also give a clue as to age. Given the probable cost of birds such as the Amazons or African Greys, it will certainly pay you not to rush into buying simply because you are impatient. The right bird will come along and it will be spending years and years with you, so curb your desire to accept any bird, because if you make a bad choice, that decision too will be with you for a very long while!

Consideration for the Parrot

The final aspect that will be covered here really is a question you should ask yourself before all else: "Am I a suitable person to own a parrot?" How many times have you seen a parrot in a cage of a home, or in a bar or similar place, that just sits there looking really dejected? These poor birds are often feather-plucked through total boredom and spend most of their pitiful lives imprisoned in a cage barely large enough to house a budgie, let along a larger parrot. They are examples of birds bought as novelties, and when the novelty dies off they are fed a little, spoken to now and then, and ignored for most of the time—other than when "friends" tap on the cage or generally annoy them in other ways that the persons think are highly amusing.

If you spend long periods away from your home or are not prepared to have your parrot loose at times (and thus risk some chewed furniture), then do not keep any of the medium- to large-sized birds; purchase a large cage and maybe have a pair of lovebirds or a pair of budgerigars—note that I said a pair, because all parrots are very social birds and very intelligent. They need company as much as they need food and should never be deprived of this.

An Orange-winged Amazon, *Amazona amazonica*. Your most important consideration when purchasing your parrot is the overall health of the bird. Your intended pet should be alert, in fine feather, and free of any discharge from the eyes and nostrils.

Accommodation

budgerigars, cockatiels and other small parrots are relatively inexpensive, whereas those needed for the large cockatoos and macaws will be very costly indeed.

Cages and Bird Stands

There is today a greater choice of cages and stands for parrots than ever before, so a visit to one or two pet shops should give you an idea of the various types. The important point regarding any cage is that it should be as large as possible and be made to a high standard. For smaller parrots, such as budgerigars and lovebirds, check that it has the metal bars going crosswise and the supports going upward (rather than the reverse), as these are better for them for clambering up and down. The door should open to form a landing platform, which is better than one which just opens in normal door fashion. The base may be of plastic or metal, and while the

The range of housing to accommodate the many parrot species is as variable, in cost terms, as is the choice of birds to occupy such. At one end of the scale, cages to house

birds may chew plastic, if they can get at an edge, it is nonetheless more hygienic. Many cages have fully removable bases, which are better for being given a really good cleaning.

Cages for larger parrots need to be robust and are better sited on a firm base, such as a square table, rather than being suspended or on single-stemmed stands. The parrot should be able to spread its wings in its cage in order to exercise them,

and the perch should be such that the bird's tail is not touching the floor (in the case of long-tailed parakeets). As all parrots should be given as much free-flying time as possible, the cage is mainly the bird's sleeping quarters, but even so is still better for being roomy.

It is possible to make one's own parrot cage today because varying sizes of welded wire that have finished edges to them can be purchased. They can be

An African Grey Parrot. Note the stainless steel feed pot, which is an excellent choice for parrot-like birds.

A Monk, or Quaker, Parakeet. In the wild, Monks construct large communal nests made of twigs.

clipped together with special clips. Be warned, however, that many parrots are very clever at undoing these clips! It therefore pays to keep an eye on these. The purchased parts can be chromed by any company that offers this service; in this way it is possible to obtain a much larger than normal cage.

Stands and Playforms

During the day parrots will enjoy being out of their cages and should be provided with a strong stand. This is essential for the larger parrots, and most come complete with food and water container, one at each end of the perch. Ideally, one or two such stands should be located in different rooms so the parrot can go to them if it is given a reasonable free run of parts of the home. Birds such as the Amazons, even if they have unclipped feathers, will often waddle along the floor rather than fly—the same is true of macaws; smaller parrots will fly from one stand to another.

I have used the word "playforms" to encompass one or more perches that are connected so that the parrot can clamber about from one to the other. They can be purchased or made to one's own ideas. If they are fitted with a ladder and a few

toys (bobbins and other similar things will be enjoyed, and destroyed, by your pet but are replaced at little or no cost), then they are better than having the bird merely perched on a stand where it can get a little bored. A final word on stands, in respect to those hideous chains one sadly sees used to restrain the parrot: Beyond being potentially very dangerous to the bird should it be alarmed and attempt to fly off, their use can never be justified. If the parrot cannot be left unattended, then it should be returned to its cage. If having both a

A pair of Blue-headed Parrots pictured outside of their nestbox.

A very tame Peach-fronted Conure, *Aratinga aurea.*

15

cage and a stand is beyond your pocket initially, then just purchase the cage and add the stand later.

Feeding Utensils

There is a wide range of feeders available from pet shops which will either be of the open pot type or of the automatic dispenser kind. The same applies to water containers. Obviously, seed and water dishes for the powerful large parrots will need to be very substantial— otherwise they will not last very long. Heavy earthenware or metal chicken feeders are often used for these birds.

A White-fronted, or Spectacled, Amazon, *Amazona albifrons*. A natural branch is an excellent means by which your pet can satisfy his urge to gnaw. Just be sure that any natural branches that are offered have not been chemically treated.

A young African Grey relishing a tasty assortment of fresh greenfoods and fruit.

Feeding

yet to be kept alive in captivity for more than the time it takes them to die from starvation!

Many pet owners still persist in assuming that all parrots, being birds, must live on a diet composed only of seeds, with an occasional piece of fruit being given to them. While it is true that many Australian parrots do consume large amounts of seed in their native habitat, it must be remembered that the greater percentage of parrots, about eighty percent, consume only a limited amount of seed in their normal diet, and the majority could survive quite well without any. Even within the same species one cannot assume that each bird will have the same food preferences, as the feeding habits within parrots in captivity must be viewed on an individual-bird basis. Another aspect that is often underrated in the feeding of most animals is the occupational and therapeutic

Few bird groups have suffered more as a result of ignorance in respect to their feeding habits than have the parrots. This fact certainly held back breeding success for many years in those species from tropical areas, and even today we have incomplete data on certain species such as the pygmy parrots, which have

A Blue-fronted Amazon chomping on a dog biscuit. Parrots of many types relish a treat food such as this.

value of various foodstuffs; in other words, beyond its nutritional value, food also serves to relax an animal and is

appear, and in order to have a better understanding of your parrot's needs it is worthwhile considering the wild state of the various species and of the reasons why captive parrots do need individual treatment.

A poor diet can contribute to a bird's suffering from stress. Pictured is an African Grey.

Australian parakeets, in the main, live in very arid country where the most prolific vegetation is seeding grasses; thus they subsist on a diet high in seed content, taking insects and fruit when the opportunity arises. In complete contrast, the parrots of South America live in areas rich in tropical plants. They have a plentiful choice of fruits, insects, and carrion, as well as of small reptiles, all of which form part of their diet. In the wild state young birds are strongly influenced in their choice of food by that which they are given by their parents, and later by what the rest of the flock is eating. If they are taken from their nests by trappers, they are usually fed a simple diet of boiled maize before being exported, while if caught as adults they will be given both maize and local fruits before export. Many adults, in fact, will hardly eat at all prior to

an important social activity that reduces the incidence of stress, thus also reducing the likelihood of illness.

Parrots are highly intelligent birds and also, unlike many other birds, have highly developed taste buds; these facts mean that they can be very selective, and stubborn, over what they will or will not eat; many will starve rather than eat foods they do not like.

It can thus be seen that feeding is a far more important subject than it may at first being exported. The imported adult is unlikely to be offered the same foods as it is accustomed to, so presents an obvious problem from the start. It may take selected seeds and fruit and continues to eat only these. It is no longer getting its original varied diet, and so is at greater risk of illness through nutritional deficiencies. Unless these birds are carefully converted to a sound diet, they either die or never attain the fitness they would normally show. The young parrots will adjust much better to a new diet because their tastes are still in a developing stage, but if they are then given a restricted menu of seed with only a few fruits and vegetables then this will become their habit; and though not a nutritionally balanced diet, it can prove difficult to persuade

them to take a wider choice of foods. As one importer may not feed his stock the same seed or fruits as another, so one finds birds of the same species having acquired differing tastes, which makes it most important that the new owner know exactly what a purchased bird is in fact eating, and then try to adjust the diet if it is considered in any way to be lacking in balance.

For the reasons outlined, it therefore pays the prospective

A Blue-fronted Amazon. Most parrots will appreciate variety in their diets. Peanuts are one of several "munchies" enjoyed by parrots, and they can be effectively used as rewards during training sessions.

owner to find out as much as possible about the habitat of the species in which one is interested, the fruits of the region, and to read as much as possible about the species as one can—before going out and purchasing a bird. The more you read on the species, the less likely you will be to be disappointed later on.

A Balanced Diet

Given the general guidelines relating to feeding habits, what then comprises a balanced diet? Various seeds figure in most parrot diets not because they are superior to other foods but simply because they are more convenient and less perishable over periods of time. The differing seeds contain variable amounts of proteins, carbohydrates, fats, minerals, and water, each of which, plus vitamins, are the essentials of sound diet. However, protein from seeds is nutritionally inferior to that from other sources, such as cheese or meat, and may lack certain amino acids that are important to sound constitutional processes. A good diet must therefore contain a wide range of foodstuffs, as in this way the chances of an essential ingredient being missing is reduced. The availability of concentrated supplements (liquid or powder) rounds out a well-planned feeding regimen.

Seed Values

It is important that all bird owners become familiar with the various constituents and uses of seed in a diet.

Carbohydrates provide energy; protein is used for bodily growth, and fats are needed to assist in physiological processes, while also being secondary sources of energy. If a bird is deficient in energy, it will convert fat into energy; once this is used up it will then convert protein to energy in order to survive—thus it will lose weight and, ultimately, perish from lack of nourishment or from disease resulting from its debilitated condition.

The smaller parrots, such as budgerigars, lovebirds, grass parakeets, and cockatiels will tend to eat the smaller seeds such as canary and the various millets—both of which are high energy seeds, and so must be supplemented with oil seeds such as rape, maw or niger to provide body-building proteins. The larger parrots will require pine nuts, peanuts, sunflower, maize, oats, and similar large-sized seeds, though they can be given the smaller seeds as well, as these will keep them occupied for quite long periods, and many birds enjoy them. The parrots of medium size, such as conures, ringnecks, and caiques, will take seeds across the whole range but will need the larger ones made softer by boiling them. Indeed, even small parrots will enjoy large seeds if these are either crushed down to an acceptable size or softened.

Parrots seem to prefer white sunflower seed to either striped or black, and when selecting this seed, choose the plump grades rather than the long thin ones. Likewise, panicum millet is more favored than either the large white or the Japanese millets. Both safflower and sesame are useful seeds to feed, the latter also having the benefit of containing vitamins A and B, which are not found in seeds other than maw.

Some breeders will not use hemp in their parrot diets in the belief that it can be harmful to the birds, but there is no evidence that would support this; and others

are unfamiliar with and also read up on it, so that you know its constituent values.

Seed Testing

It is vital that you purchase the finest seed possible, as any stored under damp conditions can be fatal if the seed has been attacked by mold or, in the case of oil seeds, if they are bruised and split, thus becoming rancid.

A perky Peach-faced Lovebird. The quality of your bird's diet will be reflected in the animal's overall condition.

use it without any problems. Oats are appreciated by many parrots either with their husk or without (called "groats"), and corn-on-the-cob is another favorite with parrots that can be purchased when plentiful and stored in a deep freeze (after blanching).

The list of potential seeds for birds is extensive, and a stock list from your local merchant is a must. Just ask the merchant about any on the list which you

Buy from a pet store that clearly has a healthy turnover in its seed—which will therefore be fresh—or from a specialist supplier to the avicultural world (these advertise in the various cage-bird magazines).

Obviously, if you have a number of birds, you will be better advised to buy seed in bulk; but do not go overboard in quantities in order to save dollars. I keep about a month's supply on hand; others hold stocks for longer periods. Available space and storage facility will be the deciding factor.

If you have any doubts about the quality of seed from a supplier, then periodic testing should be done. Place about 50 or more seeds in warm water for 48 hours, changing the water after 24 hours. Next, rinse the seeds thoroughly in a sieve, place them on absorbent paper, and put this on a tray in a warm, dark cupboard. Some 24 hours after this, the seed should start to germinate; it is then simply a case of counting the seeds that do not, and recording this data for comparison with the seed of another supplier. Do be sure in these sorts of tests that you note germinating temperature and time allowed for this; otherwise the comparisons are invalid.

Sprouting seeds not only have a higher vitamin content but also more protein value, so are favored for breeding birds and young chicks, both of which need plenty of body-building foods, rather than energy-producing seeds. For normal feeding of soaked seed the same process is followed, but the seeds are fed after being washed, prior to the germination stage.

Seed Preference

When first purchasing a parrot it is advisable to check out which seeds it has a liking for. This is done by either buying a pack of standard parrot mix and noting which seeds are taken, or by preparing your own mix of a good balance and noting those eaten. In this way, wasteful feeding of unwanted seeds will be minimized. It is not unknown for a pet parrot to be almost starving simply because its first-time-parrot-owner saw there was still plenty of seed from a parrot mix in its feed pot and assumed it was thus all right. In reality the parrot had eaten the seeds it liked and left all the others, and in effect had no seed left.

For this reason it is better to feed each kind of seed in its own container. Further, if small seeds are mixed with larger ones, then the former fall to the bottom of the feeder and do not get eaten. When two or more parrots are housed together, it is advisable to have two feeding stations (or more) in order that dominant birds do not "hog" all the choicest seeds.

When it is found that a parrot's diet in seeds has been lacking, then the newly given variety should be offered for a period even though it is ignored. Try withholding the favored seeds until later in the day. Another method is to soak the seeds or to germinate them as described earlier; in this form they may be taken, and one then works backwards to the dry seed state. If all attempts to persuade the parrot to take a given seed fail, then withdraw it from the menu and try a similar alternative. A few months later, as you modify the accepted diet, the original seed refused just may be taken. Always be an optimist!

Greenfood

There is an unlimited choice of greenfood that can be given to parrots, and every effort should be made, as with seeds, to ensure your parrot is given (and it is hoped, will accept) as wide a range as possible. Among vegetables, sprouts, cabbage, broccoli, and spinach contain 17–20mg per ounce of vitamin C, which is substantially more than is found in turnips or swedes (7mg), beet root (3mg), celery (2mg) or apple (1mg). Carrots are rich in vitamin A and also provide fiber. Peas and mung beans are other valuable greenfoods for parrots, and it is believed they will add luster to the feathers. It is worthwhile noting your bird's enthusiasm, or lack of, towards any greenfood that is given, and the time of the year. Birds are seasonal with respect to certain foods, and rejection in one month may not be so as the weather changes, or

as they come into breeding condition.

Among wild plants, chickweed is very popular though of poor food value—however, it does contain copper (a trace element needed by all animals) and seems to be liked by breeding birds. Clover has a high nutrient value, as does comfrey. Cow parsley, dandelion and mallow are other wild plants that have benefit. The problem today is that so much crop spraying is being done that care must be taken regarding plants that are collected; also, *always* wash any greenfood before it is given to the birds. Spinach can be grown in

An Orange-fronted Conure. Do not allow food to accumulate on the bottom of your pet's cage.

your garden year-round, while cress can be cultivated in window boxes to ensure a steady supply.

Among fruits, apples are the most used, but all fruits will be readily accepted by one parrot or another. Oranges, pears, bananas, grapes, pomegranates, melon, peach, and pineapple—try offering them each over a period of time to see which they prefer. Because parrots tend to be wasteful eaters, it is best to offer a limited amount as a mixed salad, and to cut the fruits into segments. With the smaller parrots, fruit can be attached to the aviary wire with clips, and this will keep them happy.

Supplements

There are now a number of powdered and liquid high-vitamin concentrates available for birds, as well as vitaminized tonic seeds, and these can be useful if your parrot accepts only a very limited range of foodstuffs. Powders can be sprinkled onto fruit, while liquid can be added to the drinking water.

Your pet dealer can show you a number of commercially prepared supplements and additives.

Minerals

These are vital to the welfare of your birds, and grit is essential too; it can be purchased in packets and given in small pots for the smaller parrots, and sprinkled on the cage or aviary floor for the larger species. Without this the bird is unable to grind up its seed—for, remember, birds have no teeth, so mastication is effected in the stomach by the muscles and grit. Oyster shell is a good source of lime, as is cuttlefish bone, which can be purchased from your local pet store.

Water

A constant supply of fresh drinking water should always be available to birds. If they have a well-balanced diet containing ample fruits, then they may take little water, but it should still be there so they have the choice.

Breeding

If one keeps aviary parrots, as opposed to single pet birds, then it will not be long before the desire to breed one's stock becomes strong. It is a wonderful sensation to see the first youngsters one breeds emerge from their nest box and make their maiden flights. Also, every clutch of parrots that is reared helps those in the wild to remain in their natural habitat. Each year millions of birds are trapped for export to the world's pet markets, and only by building up large stocks of aviary-bred birds does the demand for wild-caught stock start to decline.

The classic case to illustrate this is of course the budgerigar—all birds sold through pet shops are home bred, the Australian government having banned the export of its fauna many years ago. The same is true of other Australian parakeets, so species that were once very expensive are now available at reasonable prices. Conversely, South American parrots and the large cockatoos of Australia, which are much more difficult to breed,

Also included in the group of popular pet birds is the Peach-faced Lovebird. A mated pair can be a true delight to their owner.

command extremely high prices. This does not mean that the newcomer to parrots should go out and purchase the rarer, high-priced birds in the hope of making some big dollars from breeding with them. Would that

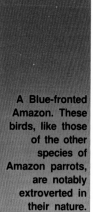

A Blue-fronted Amazon. These birds, like those of the other species of Amazon parrots, are notably extroverted in their nature.

it were so easy!

Any person purchasing parrots in the hope of making a lot of money from their breeding will be sadly disappointed. You should only breed parrots if you are interested in them for their beauty and intelligence.

This established, then the next question must be, Which are the best birds to start with? The answer to this is most

definitely those which are well-established breeders, reasonably priced, and which will not pose problems of compatibility. The list would include budgerigars, cockatiels, Bourke's Parakeets, Red-rumps, Elegants, and numerous other small Australian grass parakeets. Lovebirds and their South American equivalents, the parrotlets, would be short-tailed alternatives to the long-tailed varieties stated. In all of these species consideration has been given to the size of the aviary needed and to their noise level. Numerous conures and Asiatic parakeets are reasonably priced but need more spacious accommodation and can be very noisy—which will not endear you to your neighbors.

By commencing with popular varieties, you can build up experience of parrot husbandry without the risk of expensive birds dying on you for no other reason than your lack of bird-keeping knowledge. Further, there will be many more breeders in your area to advise you when you have a problem. This is not likely to be the case if you attempt to start off with high-priced birds.

Aviary-bred birds are much more reliable breeders than wild-caught specimens and will be well acclimatized. Other than budgerigars and cockatiels, it is not advised that parrots be bred on a colony system; they should be housed on their own as a breeding pair. Even the two mentioned will need to be kept as pairs if one wishes to exercise control over which birds mate with which in order that exhibition birds or particular colors are produced. It is also recommended that you start with just one, or maybe two, species; very often beginners get carried away by the desire to have lots of pairs of many species, but this is a poor way of breeding as it restricts potential alternative mates on hand, as well as reducing the chances of foster parents being available if needed. A minimum of three pairs— unrelated— would be a

sound number to start with.

Sexing

The popular parrots such as cockatiels, budgerigars, certain lovebirds, and small parakeets are sexually dimorphic, which means the cock and hen are visually different; many larger parrots are not, so obtaining a true pair is not always easy. In

A Blue-fronted Amazon perching trustfully on his owner's hand. Before beginning a breeding program, consider carefully whether or not you have the time and resources to devote to such an endeavor.

the latter cases many birds advertised for sale have been sexed by surgical means and so present no problems. The veterinarian will make a small incision in the bird's flank and insert a probe with which he can see the sexual organs; he can also tell whether the birds are in breeding condition. He also is able to inspect other internal organs at the same time, so in this regard modern bird keepers are at a great advantage over those of yesteryear.

Compatibility

When pairs are introduced to each other, they should always be watched until you are sure they are compatible. In most species, it is the cock that is dominant, but this is reversed in Asiatic parakeets. If the cock is overly aggressive, he should be removed and tried again a few days later. If the pair just do not get on at all, then alternative mates will need to be found. Because of this aspect it is always a good idea to introduce prospective mates some weeks, or even months, before breeding is due to take place. In the case of the very large parrots the pair bond can be very strong—but equally it may take months, or even years, for the bond to develop to the stage where they will settle down to rear chicks.

Nest Boxes

Only when both birds of a pair are in full breeding condition, which means they are well-exercised, very fit and neither over- nor under-weight, should

the nest boxes be installed. These will usually provide the stimulus for them to mate. Place the boxes at convenient height where you can inspect them daily, and preferably in a shaded spot. In the case of colony breeding of budgerigars or cockatiels, a number of boxes in excess of the number of pairs will be needed—and all placed at about the same height so there is no squabbling for prime sites. Any birds that fail to pair up should be removed, as they will likely unsettle those which are breeding.

Of course, budgies, cockatiels, lovebirds, and other small parrots will breed in large cages in a bird room, but the vast majority of parrots will need an aviary for the best results.

NEST BOX DESIGN. There are many styles used by breeders for differing species, but the essentials are that the box be stoutly made from thick wood so that it will withstand changes in the weather. Its size will reflect the size of the birds, and, as a guide, the base should be roughly square and have a width equivalent to the body length of the hen (but not including her tail length). Grandfather-clock shapes are favored for many larger parakeets, while old barrels are often used for the large macaws and cockatoos.

Smaller parrot nest boxes can have a wooden concave placed in them so the eggs are retained together, but no nesting material need be included, as parrots will make their own from pieces of wood and their feathers. A few bits of branch can be placed in the nest box, and this might induce the hen to commence breeding. In larger boxes, a few slats of wood should be fixed to the inside, below the entrance hole, so that the hen can exit with ease. Some breeders use welded mesh for this, but it is not unknown for hens and chicks to get their claws caught in this, so there is the potential damage being caused to the birds.

With larger parrots, it is advised that extra pieces of wood be fixed inside the nest box and these will be gnawed by the hen to prepare a base; if these are not provided, she will probably start reducing the nest box to match wood! The entrance hole should be made just large enough for the hen to get in; if she wants it larger she will attend to this herself, and it is good for her to do just that. A landing perch should be placed just beneath the hole, on the outside.

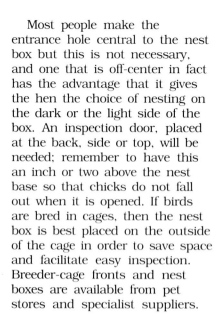

Most people make the entrance hole central to the nest box but this is not necessary, and one that is off-center in fact has the advantage that it gives the hen the choice of nesting on the dark or the light side of the box. An inspection door, placed at the back, side or top, will be needed; remember to have this an inch or two above the nest base so that chicks do not fall out when it is opened. If birds are bred in cages, then the nest box is best placed on the outside of the cage in order to save space and facilitate easy inspection. Breeder-cage fronts and nest boxes are available from pet stores and specialist suppliers.

Feeding

It is most important that in the build-up weeks to egg laying that the hen in particular is given extra foods in her diet. She will need more oil seeds so the eggs will provide the embryos with a good protein base to grow on; she will need bread and milk or a calcium supplement to ensure that the chicks do not suffer from rickets, this being in addition to the cuttlefish bone or oyster shell already provided throughout the year.

Egg Laying

The hen will lay eggs on alternate days, and she will commence, in most cases, to incubate once the second egg has been laid. The number of eggs in a clutch will obviously vary both from bird to bird and species to species. All parrot eggs are white, and size varies according to the species.

EGG BINDING. This distressing condition is seen when a hen is unable to pass an egg. The cause is usually an out-of-condition or overweight bird or a soft-shelled egg, which is the result of a mineral deficiency in the hen's diet. What happens is that the muscles of the hen's body are not able to push the egg along the oviduct because of her physical state or because the soft egg "gives" when her muscles contract. Unless the egg is removed quite quickly, the hen will die.

The usual procedure is to place the hen in a warm spot, such as a cage with an infrared lamp at one end on the outside. If this fails, then gently lubricate the hen's vent with petroleum jelly and hold her over steam from a pan of water (but not so that she is likely to be scalded!) for a few seconds at a time. This may relax her organs so that the egg is expelled. If these efforts fail, call your veterinarian immediately. Do not attempt to remove the egg yourself, for if it breaks the hen will most certainly be lost.

DEAD-IN-SHELL. It sometimes happens that chicks die in their shell, and the reason is usually because the egg was too dry or, the opposite, where the humidity was such that the egg failed to lose water and the chick was in effect drowned in the shell. The incidence of these cases is greater in birds bred indoors than those in aviaries. Other cases of unhatched eggs are usually due to the fact that they ere not fertilized by the male through his lack of condition. Such eggs are termed "clear," and a bright light shone from below them will show this, compared with fertile eggs, which get darker as the embryo develops.

DAMAGED EGGS. Sometimes eggs will be found broken in the nest, or which there are many possible causes. Hens sense when things are amiss and will attempt to remove any dead-in-shell birds; they will also break eggs that they know are in some way not right, so it is not always a case that one has a less-than-ideal

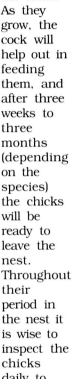

mother. Keep notes on such happenings, as on all aspects of breeding, and in this way you may well be able eventually to discover the reasons for such occurrences. It is always worthwhile having eggs and dead chicks examined by the veterinarian, who may be able to advise of the cause and thus help you avoid such disasters in the future.

Chick Rearing
After hatching, the chicks will rapidly gain weight, and by the time they leave the nest they will be almost as heavy as their parents. Initially they are fed by the hen, who is brought food by her mate. As they grow, the cock will help out in feeding them, and after three weeks to three months (depending on the species) the chicks will be ready to leave the nest. Throughout their period in the nest it is wise to inspect the chicks daily to ensure they are being fed—this will be evident from their swollen crops. The eminent parrot authorities, such as George Smith and Rosemary Low, advise that daily weighing of chicks can often avert problems, as the babies' weight gains can be plotted and predicted. If one is suddenly found not to be gaining

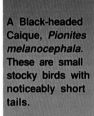

A Black-headed Caique, *Pionites melanocephala*. These are small stocky birds with noticeably short tails.

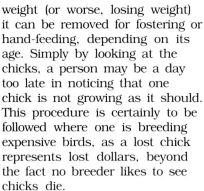

weight (or worse, losing weight) it can be removed for fostering or hand-feeding, depending on its age. Simply by looking at the chicks, a person may be a day too late in noticing that one chick is not growing as it should. This procedure is certainly to be followed where one is breeding expensive birds, as a lost chick represents lost dollars, beyond the fact no breeder likes to see chicks die.

Once the chicks are seen to be feeding on their own, they should be removed to separate quarters; otherwise there is a real risk they will be attacked and killed by their parents, especially by the cock. Many parrots will commence laying a second round of eggs while chicks are still in the nest. Therefore special attention must be paid to the parents in case of attacks, in which case the eggs or the chicks should be removed, again depending on the age of the babies. Some species are more notorious than others in this aspect of attacking their own young, but with parrots one cannot specify hard-and-fast rules; they must all be treated on their own merits as no two are quite the same.

Bird Friends

Irrespective of how much reading one does on the subject of breeding, there is no adequate replacement for actual experience. When your birds lay their first eggs is the time you begin to worry if things are as they should be. This is the time when an experienced aviculturist

friend is a boon! For this reason it certainly pays to join your local bird club. You may then be able to visit a member's aviary to see young chicks in the nest and generally pick up useful advice. Further, your friends will no doubt be only too willing to visit you when your big moment arrives and check over things with you to see everything is well and that you can go to bed in the full knowledge "your" new babies are quite happy!

Leg Banding

It is often desirable to be able to identify various birds in a collection, especially in instances where juveniles rapidly attain adult plumage and are housed with older birds. This is effected by means of leg bands (also called "rings"), which are available in metal or plastic, closed or split. They are purchased from specialist suppliers and can be colored or numbered. A closed ring is placed on a chick at about five to six days of age. Be sure to request a ring for the species in question, and if it is too loose then try it again a few days later. The two forward-facing toes and one of the rear toes are eased through the ring and then, with the help of a match stick or the like, the remaining toe is gently pulled through. Plastic rings can be used on the smallest parrots but would soon be destroyed by most others. Rings are not actually the ideal means of identification, as the bird can get caught up on them, but until tattooing or other better methods are developed, they are the best available at this time. I have seen various other methods used, such as a dab of paint on the beak (in larger parrots), feathers dyed with a stain, and tail feathers trimmed on youngsters, but none of these is as permanent as ringing.

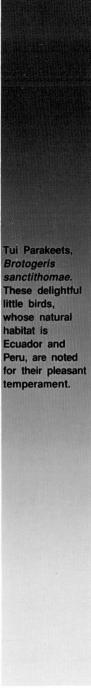

Tui Parakeets, *Brotogeris sanctithomae.* These delightful little birds, whose natural habitat is Ecuador and Peru, are noted for their pleasant temperament.

The Pet Parrot

Contrary to what is often claimed, a parrot is far from the ideal pet as far as the average household is concerned. They are very demanding of one's time, they do not always accept the attentions of every member of the family, and they are capable of considerable damage to the home—and can make the sort of noise that will make you wish you had bought a goldfish. Further, you will need to think in terms of what will befall your pet when you die, as in many cases it will certainly outlive you. If you have been the ideal owner to such a bird, will it enjoy in its old age the life *you* would have given it?

Parrots can be very inconvenient at times, so why, with all these negatives, do people keep them? The fact is, about half of all the larger parrots kept in homes are unsuited to them, which is why so many change hands so quickly, or end up as ignored ornaments in the corner of the room.

Wild-Caught Adults

One reason why many parrots are unsuited to a home is that they are wild-caught adults. Their age when caught will determine whether they can ever attain any degree of tameness. A young adult can be tamed, but it needs the attention of a very caring and patient owner. Most wild adults end up being passed from one owner or dealer to another until, hopefully, they are purchased by someone who wants them as aviary birds; however, even here they may prove unsuitable for breeding if too old, so they may then continue on this sad merry-go-round. Birds that have proved poor breeders, or which are known to be bad feather pluckers of their young, or to be very aggressive to their mates, may all end up advertised as pets. You can see that selecting a bird is no easy matter, as it is often impossible to verify statements made by the seller who might himself have been deceived when the bird was purchased. Regardless of species, any bird required as a pet *must* be young if it is ever to become a well-adjusted member of a household; ideally, it should come from a breeder so its age is not in doubt.

Many tame and talking birds are seen in pet stores and may well be genuine and have been sold by owners who, for one reason or another, had to part with them; some however, may have a quirk in their makeup. Maybe they have moments when they scream loudly, and this is the reason for their being sold or they may have proved too boisterous for their owners. Such birds are quite normal, and it is a case of the owners clearly not having been aware of what parrot owning entailed.

Choice of Species

For the average household certain parrots are not recommended. For example, the larger macaws and cockatoos will prove very destructive and very noisy and are certainly not birds for first-time owners. Let us start at the opposite end with

the smaller parrots such as budgies, lovebirds, and cockatiels. Each of these will make charming pets and are not noisy. If acquired when straight from the nest they will become very tame and may even learn a few words. They will live from nine years upward, cockatiels sometimes attaining ages in excess of 30 years. If you would like a parrot but know you will not have the time to devote to the larger birds, then purchase a pair of these smaller birds and they will be good company for each other when you are not at home. It is always sad to see a single budgerigar or cockatiel, as these are very social birds that live in large flocks. Many of the conures make delightful pets but can be rather noisy. It is generally felt that long-tailed parakeets, such as ringnecks, do not make good pets, but this is a view I do not hold. One of my favorite birds was an Alexandrine Ringneck acquired as a young adult. After two years of careful attention he had become a most charming and tame bird and was given the liberty of our home. Ringnecks

A striking African Ringneck Parakeet, *Psittacula krameri*. These birds can make very good pets if they are hand-reared when they are babies.

may not be as amusing as some parrots but can be very confiding pets. Again, Australian parakeets are not regarded as suited to the home environment, but a number of the smaller species, such as Bourke's and Elegants, are found in Australian homes and appear to make delightful pets in much the same way as does the cockatiel. The advantage of many of the well-established breeding species is that they are reasonably priced and can be purchased as babies, so you are sure on this important account.

Amazon parrots are of course very popular, as is the African Grey. These birds will need a great deal of attention but make very rewarding pets, the Amazons in particular being highly amusing. Greys are the finest of all parrots as talkers, but *never* purchase a parrot for this reason only, as chances are you will be very disappointed. Few match up to expectations, while many never talk and then others do so only after much teaching. Some will learn words and sounds without any instruction, but the beauty of parrots lies in their individual characters, not in talking potential. Greys become attached to individuals rather than whole families and can be quite aggressive to strangers who approach them. In this sense Amazons are better.

Siting the Cage

The ideal position for a parrot cage is close to a wall near a window in your main living room. Parrots need to be in the center of activities, where they can see and hear all that is going on. You must treat them as very much one of the family if you want to get the best from them as pets. Never place the cage where it will be in direct sunlight so that the bird cannot escape the sun's rays; in the wild they would be sheltered by dense foliage. They must be free from drafts, and being near to a wall will give them a sense of security on that side, and people will pass only in front of them.

Home or Prison?

It has been stated earlier that a cage should be as large as possible, but here more can be added on this aspect. A bird having a smaller cage but ample liberty time is far better off than one in a very large cage but allowed no time out of it. The cage should be a place to sleep and retire for privacy; if it is, your pet will return to it of its own choosing; if it is not, then it becomes a prison cell which it cannot wait to get free of.

Parrots given a great deal of time out of their cage will spend much time either sitting on the top of it, on their feeding station (if one is supplied), or on some other vantage point where they can see what is going on. They will of course also spend much time generally investigating and getting into mischief if you are not watching them, and will spend much time on your shoulder or arm, depending on their likes (my Alexandrine preferred to sit on my head when watched television).

Do They Bite?

All parrots bite, and bites of the larger ones can be very painful when they do. If you are at all nervous about being bitten by a medium-sized bird (say an Amazon) then perhaps you should reconsider acquiring one. This said, a family pet rarely bites and usually will do so only when annoyed about being moved against its will. They will sometimes also nibble your ear or nose harder than they realize. It therefore pays to have a short, stout stick (broom-handle thickness) so that if your pet must be put in its cage, and it does not agree with you on this account, you offer it the stick to stand on rather than your hand. In this way the stick will get a hard bite, but Polly will stand on it and both parties are happy! It must be remembered that parrots are capable of showing all the same emotions as humans—love, hate, jealousy and anger—which is why so many people find them irresistible companions.

We test things with our hands and feet, whereas parrots use their beaks for this purpose. Often people think a parrot is about to bite them when it is merely going to test their finger. This is especially true when they are first being finger-tamed. If the parrots feel secure, they will then stand on it. Once tame, they will alight on it as soon as it is placed near to their breast. Some birds "test" much harder than others, so it is a case of

knowing the individual bird.

Bathing

It is very important that all parrots be able to bathe, as in this way their feathers are kept in fine fettle. Small birds will preen themselves from a receptacle such as a shallow dish; others prefer to be sprayed. The medium-to-large birds prefer the latter. On warm days a parrot can be taken into the garden if there is a shower, and it will enjoy this, extending and shaking its feathers. Some owners even give their birds a shower in the bathroom, while others simply use a mister used for spraying plants. Your pet's feathers should be sprayed twice a week in order that they are kept in healthy condition.

Other Pets

Parrots will get along quite well with cats and dogs, provided they are supervised at all times. It is foolhardy to take chances by leaving a parrot alone in a room

Peach-fronted Conure. Although members of this species tend to be rather noisy, they can make very affectionate pets.

containing a dog or cat—
especially if it is a small parrot
such as a budgerigar, lovebird or
cockatiel. Should you have fish
in your room, then ensure that
the tank has a canopy over it so
the bird cannot accidentally fall
in and drown. It is not
recommended that two parrots,
such as Amazons, Greys or
similar-sized birds be kept
together as pets unless both
were acquired together as
youngsters. If a second pet is
introduced into the house of an
established bird, then the
chances are that the older parrot
will be jealous of the newcomer
and will take the first
opportunity to attack it. This is
not so with smaller parrots, but
even they need to be watched
initially to see that they are
compatible.

Dangers

When the bird is at liberty, all
the possible escape routes and
danger points must be
considered. For example,
chimney openings should be
covered and exhaust fans should
be turned off and their openings
closed. Kitchen burners should
be turned off if the parrot is in
the kitchen, though this is one
room where your pet should *not*
be allowed. Telephone and
electric wires are other potential
hazards to your birds, as are
electric heaters of the non-
convector type; even a pot of hot
tea is a possible danger point for
an inquisitive bird. When a bird
is given liberty in a room for the
first time, and if its wings are
unclipped, then it may fly

straight into the window glass,
so draw the curtains or
otherwise hang some netting so
that injury to the bird is
prevented. You are advised to
remove any valuable ornaments
and other items that your pet
might render to becoming ex-
valuables!

Egg Laying

It sometimes happens that a
female pet bird will lay eggs; she
need not have been mated to do
this. Of course, they will be
"clear" and unfertilized. They
should not be removed; the hen
should be allowed to lay her
normal clutch and attempt to
incubate them. Eventually, she
will ignore them, and they can
be removed. If they are taken
from her as she lays them, she
will lay more than she should—
and this could result in a serious
calcium deficiency and even
death. It is also very stressful to
her if the eggs are removed, so
let nature take its course.

Taming

It has been stressed that only
young birds should be
purchased if you want them to
be really tame. In such cases the
chances are, especially if they
have been hand-reared, that
they will already be finger tame.
If, however, they are young birds
not already tame, then you will
have to attend to this—but there
is great satisfaction from
achieving this and recognizing
the confidence the bird must
have in you for it to be done.
There are many ways of taming
birds, and authorities differ on

the most successful one. Some advocate the use of gloves and sticks; others advise letting the bird come to you when at liberty; some prefer to clip the bird's wings first; others do not.

For myself, I do not say my way is superior, only that for me it has always proven successful. Whether or not the wings are clipped does not bother me simply because the taming is effected largely while the bird is caged. I have no time for the use of gloves. Parrots are *not* birds of prey, and they are very intelligent. The most crucial aspect of hand-taming is that the bird should overcome its fear of humans and be aware that a hand does not feel like a bit of wood—or a leather glove.

When the bird is first acquired, it should be left alone in its cage for a few days so that it becomes familiar with its new surroundings and owner. It should be spoken to quietly and often, and all movements near its cage should be slow and deliberate. Initially, it will tend to retreat to the bars of the cage when approached; but when it stops doing this, the time is ripe for it to be offered a favored tidbit through the cage bars. Again, at first, it will not approach you, but if you hold the treat in your fingers for a few minutes and sit very still, it will become curious sooner or later and will take the treat and retreat quickly. In other cases one might have to drop the treat to the cage floor a few times until the bird knows what you are holding. It will eventually come to you, but how long this process takes varies from bird to bird. Offer the treat from the end of the perch so the bird need only walk along this and can retreat quickly back along it.

Once the parrot takes the food without problem and does not retreat but eats it where it stands and looks for more, then it is time to move to the side of the cage door and offer it through the bars. Now, the bird is making much more of an effort to come to you. Continue for a few times in this way before going on to the next step: opening the door and holding the treat very still in your fingers. The bird will become cautious again but will come, slowly. Never try to rush the taming process.

Once the bird will readily take the treat from your hand at the cage door, then place the hand further into the cage. Next is the moment of truth! Hold your finger across the line of the bird, like a perch, and just above its leg level (birds never step down, only up). Be very still, and the bird will bend over and test your finger, hopefully not too hard. It may step onto it or it may retreat to the bars; no matter, you are gaining its confidence. Repeat this many times until the bird will stand on your finger.

Now you can open the cage door and wait for the parrot to come to the entrance itself and alight on your hand. It will probably then fly off into the room, but you have achieved ninety percent of the taming, as you will be able to retrieve it via your hand rather than having to dim the lights and place a towel over it, which is the best way if you have allowed it immediate liberty before taming. When a bird is first let loose, it is invariably very nervous, so after a few moments it will gladly step back onto your hand, as this represents security to it. When it does, talk very quietly to it and move very slowly back to its cage where it will go in (usually!). Sometimes it might alight on the cage but will then climb back into the cage itself, especially if you put a tidbit inside.

When a parrot first sits on your shoulder, it is very curious about your hair, ears, and nose and will nibble at these to feel what they are like. Do not be afraid as the nibble will rarely hurt—that might come later when the bird is really very confident in you and gets cheeky or excited! Parrots (the medium-to-large ones) are like children, as they become very tame and do get naughty. They are very bright and respond to being told off. If they nip too hard, gently tap their beaks and say no. They quickly learn. I have always found the best time to tame parrots is in the evening, when no one else is around and only when I know I have plenty of time to devote to the bird.

Talking

Again, this should be done in total quietness so the bird is not distracted from what you are saying to it. Commence with simple words at first and repeat these many, many times. Once the bird says its first word, and this can range from days to not at all, then add to its vocabulary; as this grows, small phrases can be put together. Teach it your name so that when it sees you it will say "Hello, James" or whatever—this is much better than teaching it to say its own name. A parrot will mimic many sounds; a Mealy Amazon I owned had previously been kept with children and chickens, both of which it could imitate at will—regrettably, in its repertoire was a screaming child! The same bird was superb at repeating the songs of the various other birds we kept in our store, and fabulously interpreted our telephone conversations.

Feather Clipping

One advantage of feather clipping is that the bird is much easier to retrieve when it is in the taming process. Further, should it be allowed, or get, out into your garden it can again be recaptured without too much problem. Clipped feathers will be replaced at the next molt. Either the feathers of both wings can be clipped or just from one wing—the latter resulting in a curved flight which tends to discourage the bird from flying. There is really no need to clip a pet bird's feathers, but if this is considered a necessity then take your pet to an experienced vet or parrot keeper who will show you how to do it.

Provided parrots are given a great deal of affection, they will make quite enchanting and rewarding pets, and they need

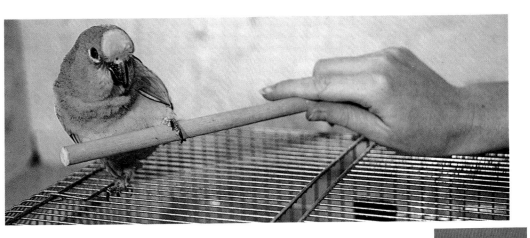

not be the larger expensive kinds, for a lovebird has all the virtues of a big bird but just happens to be very small—which can be a decided advantage on many occasions. Take a long, thoughtful look before you decide on exactly which species is suited to your needs.

43

Health

A Yellow-faced Parrotlet, *Forpus xanthops*, exhibiting every outward sign of good health.

If parrots are given a proper balanced diet, accommodated in clean, draft-free aviaries or cages, and their feathers kept in fine condition by bathing, then they should live trouble-free lives. However, even the best kept of stock can become ill, as many diseases are airborne and keepers who have numerous birds may introduce an ailment when adding fresh stock to their collection. Generally, house pets are less prone to illness than are their aviary counterparts.

It is essential that general cleanliness be of the highest order. Cages and aviaries must be cleaned thoroughly at least once every week, loose seed should be removed daily, and in the case of caged birds, their floor litter should be replaced daily. Always wash your hands after handling a bird and keep all feeder pots well cleaned.

The more you are acquainted with your birds, the more rapidly you will notice any little changes in their behavior—and these might be the first signs of illness. Birds normally rest on one leg, with their heads tucked back, feathers fluffed. If they are seen using two legs while resting, then chances are they are not feeling so good. Watch their droppings so you know what is normal for each bird. Loose droppings are not in themselves danger signs, for if birds are given correct fruit rations this will result in more viscous feces. However, very wet feces may indicate a problem.

Swollen or stained vents, puffed eyelids, heavy breathing, reduced appetite, and general lethargy all tell you the bird is ailing.

The minute you sense a bird is off color, it should be isolated from other stock and placed in a cage where a higher temperature can be maintained 30°C (85°F). This alone will cure many minor disorders. Place an infrared lamp above or in front of the cage, and at one end of it. In this way the bird can move from the hottest point to a lower temperature to suit itself. A thermometer is a *must*, so the lamp can be positioned to maintain the required temperature. Extra heat will make the bird more thirsty, so ensure there is always water present, and into this can be put antibiotics as per your veterinarian's instructions. The bird should still be given its normal food rations; if it refuses these, give it favored tidbits. It is essential that it eats something, as small birds will die overnight of starvation while larger ones may be able to last only forty-eight hours without eating. If needed, the patient may have to be force-fed by tube or dropper—but your vet will do this and instruct you if such drastic measures are needed.

Once the illness has been identified, you should obviously ensure that its cause is eliminated, to prevent further outbreaks. Many disorders stem from a diet where fouled food has been consumed, or where there is a lack of a needed vitamin or mineral in the diet.

Other causes may be of parasitic origin through unclean accommodation, or secondary infection resulting from parasitic causes which have reduced the bird's ability to fight off what might normally have been only a minor disorder.

A bird is more likely to succumb to illness when it is under stress, so it is at greater risk when freshly imported, when being installed in a new environment, during the breeding season, and when in molt. At such times it should not only be left quietly alone but also be given extra vitamin supplements and, in the case of imported birds, not placed in outside aviaries until it has become fully acclimatized.

Any bird that has been hospitalized should not be returned to its quarters until the higher temperature it has been in has been reduced to normal

A Mitred Conure, *Aratinga mitrata.* Following the basic rules of good husbandry will be very effective in keeping your pet healthy.

45

over one or two days—longer if needed.

Given these basic guidelines, most problems will be avoided, but the following are those most often encountered.

Cuts

These may arise from a fight, getting caught on a wire or a similar object. Apply a styptic pencil, alum solution or similar substance. Most wounds quickly heal, but should they be of a serious nature, then wrap the bird in a towel and take it to the vet immediately.

Digestive Problems

This can cover a multitude of diseases, which can range from minor stomach upsets to salmonellosis—a potentially serious infection that can be transmitted to humans. Isolate birds with signs of diarrhea, and take a sample of the feces to your vet for laboratory examination. Reduce the greenfood given but ensure that water is in constant supply.

Feather Plucking

A hen will sometimes pluck the feathers of young chicks, but unless she takes this to extremes it will not be a problem—but she should be watched on this account. In severe cases, remove the chicks and place them with the cock, who will continue to feed them. Alternatively, they can be hand-reared. Plucking of an adult by itself is usually the result of boredom or a diet deficiency. At the first signs of this, seek the opinion of a parrot breeder, who may be able to tell if you are feeding incorrectly. In the case of a bored bird, overcoming the problem is more difficult, and the best solution is to find someone who will give the bird aviary space in which to exercise itself. Some birds in aviaries become habitual pluckers of their mates and should be removed to separate accommodation—sometimes, luckily, a change of aviary and surroundings cures the problem.

Lice and Mites

These parasites are the result of unhygienic housing. Red mites will live in crevices and come out at night to feed on the blood of birds. Lice remain on the host. When these are seen, treatment involves an aerosol available from your pet store. This will quickly eradicate the pests, but all accommodation—especially nest boxes—will also need to be treated; repeat treatments as prescribed by the manufacturer will be needed to kill off unhatched eggs.

Vitamin Deficiency

It is generally held that a great number of avian disorders stem from lack of vitamins. For example, in lorikeets an especially troublesome ailment known as moniliasis is the result of a fungus mold growing inside the mouth. This is the result of a vitamin A deficiency. The best way of ensuring that your birds lack no vitamins is to feed one of the proprietary multivitamin preparations for birds.

Parrots for Beginners

New World Parrots—Conures

This group of birds consists of 43 species in eight genera, and they are rather like miniature macaws. In past years they were always more popular in the USA than in Europe, but this is now changing, as is their establishment as breeders. Indeed, most species available can become prolific, once they have settled into their accommodation. As with the macaws, the sexes are similar, so surgical sexing is recommended. Conures can be colony bred, providing they have a large area where they can defend their own nest site; allow 2m (6ft 6in) per pair for this. Of course, like macaws, their problem is that they are very noisy, so you might not be popular with your neighbors; it would not be unknown for complaints to be upheld by local authorities, so it is as well you ponder this aspect first. Some birds are relatively quiet but this cannot be known in advance. They prefer darkened nest sites, and the nest box may be of the type used for cockatiels or of the grandfather-clock style—individuals vary in their preference. There is no doubt

47

that numerous species will one day become as well known as many Australian parakeets because conures have the advantage that they may make superb pets.

They can also be bred in cages much as are lovebirds, so they have much going for them. They are more expensive than cockatiels or even the popular small Australian parakeets, but even so they are still within the range of most of us—other than the yellow varieties which can be costly, especially the magnificent Golden, or Queen of Bavaria, Conure, *Aratinga guarouba*, which has a length of 36cm (14in).

Often offered for sale is the Peach-fronted Conure, *A. aurea*, 26cm (10in). This parrot is known in the UK as the Golden-crowned. Similar is the Petz's, or

A Peach-fronted Conure, *A. aurea*, one of the more commonly available conure species.

Halfmoon, Conure, *A. canicularis*, which is also known as the Orange-fronted. In fact the two are often confused, but the former has a black beak whereas the latter has one of an ivory shade, with only the lower being black. Another species often available is the Mitred Conure, *A. mitrata*, which is not unlike the Wagler's Conure, *A. wagleri*.

Undoubtedly the most popular conure is the Nanday, *Nandayus nenday*, which is 31cm (12in). It is the only member of its genus and is a prolific breeder. These make affectionate pets and can often be purchased at very reasonable prices—up to half that of other conures. Parrots of the genus *Pyrrhura* are possibly quieter than those of *Aratinga*, so are gaining in popularity. If you like a colorful bird, then check out the White-eared Conure, *Pyrrhura leucotis*, 23cm (9in) and the Crimson-bellied Conure, *P. rhodogaster*. These are delightful little birds. The last conure to be mentioned is the Red-bellied, *P. frontalis*, for, while not as colorful as others, it has a quiet beauty, but is also more often on sale than other species.

Parakeets

There are a number of attractive parakeets that have been exported from South America over the years, yet few have been bred on any scale, other than the Quaker, or Monk, Parakeet, *Myiopsitta monachus*. This bird of 29cm (11in) has proved so prolific that wild populations have become established in the USA, the UK, Austria, and in other countries. A feature of it is that it builds large communal nests of twigs and is a very raucous bird. Single pairs will use a normal nest box. It is well recommended to beginners. Blue and yellow mutations are known but command high prices. The lack of color, together with their rather shrill voices, no doubt accounts for few South American parakeets being bred.

Of those often on sale the Lineolated, *Bolborhynchus lineola*, is an exception and is well-established in aviaries. It is a quiet bird that breeds well on a colony system. It is a very peaceful bird and is an excellent one for the novice. A species that is quite colorful is the Gold-fronted, or Mountain, Parakeet, *B. aurifrons*, 18cm (7in), but it has not proved prolific. Other species seen will be the White-winged, *Brotogeris versicolorus*, also known as the Canary-winged (a subspecies); the Orange-winged, *B. pyrrhopterus*; the Tovi, or Bee-bee, *B. jugularis;* and the Tui Parakeet, *B. sanctithomae*. These range between 17–23cm (7–9in) and have been imported in very large numbers in the past, mostly for sale as pet birds. In all, there are 13 species of parakeets found in the three genera.

Parrotlets

This group of 15 species is found in three genera. They are an attractive group of small, short-tailed parrots that might be regarded as being the South American equivalent of the African lovebirds. They range in size from 12–13cm (4.5–5in) with one species being 14.5cm (5.5 in); thus they are slightly smaller than lovebirds and have somewhat smaller beaks. Sexes are dimorphic, the hen not exhibiting the blue found in males. However, obtaining true pairs can be difficult because the females of the different species are similar, so only when young males have fledged can one see if they resemble their fathers; if not, then it is probable the

A pair of Orange-fronted Conures.

A watchful Mitred Conure. Not many birds of this species exhibit the red markings of such intensity as are visible on this bird's abdomen.

female was of another species.

For breeding it is suggested that pairs are given a budgerigar-style nest box, though the handy person could make one slightly smaller than normal, which these birds appear to prefer. They can be cage bred but tend to fight, and they can be colony bred. As with lovebirds, they should not be housed in mixed aviaries unless with larger birds, as they can be quite aggressive. Young birds straight from the nest make engaging little pets which are not noisy.

As a group, they have not proved as popular as lovebirds as they do not have the range of colors, and lovebirds have also many established mutations.

The most readily available parrotlet is the Celestial, *Forpus coelestis*, while the most vivid is the Yellow-faced, *F. xanthops*. In all cases it is suggested that chicks be removed from parents as soon as they are feeding, as they are otherwise at risk of being attacked by the adults.

Amazon Parrots

The Amazon parrots are probably the most desired birds for pet owners, and this is not surprising since, if acquired when young, they are talented mimics, the right size to be carried about, and very amusing. They are probably the most extroverted of all parrots. There are 27 species in the genus *Amazona*, and, of these, seven are island species, the remainder frequenting habitats from Mexico to Argentina. Size varies from the Yellow-billed (Red-throated), *Amazona collaria*, at 28cm (11in) to the Imperial, *A. imperialias*, at 45cm (17in). Availability varies simply because Amazons exported a number of years ago will be offered for sale from time to time—well after the country of origin has imposed export bans. In all cases prices are high.

Considerably more are kept in the USA than in Europe, and American breeders have been more successful than those in other countries. In particular, Ramon Noegel has had unequaled success in his Florida aviaries with Cuban Amazons, and is a shining example of just how important a role the aviculturist can have in the preservation and breeding of endangered species.

At this time, the lowest-priced Amazon is likely to be the Orange-winged, *A. amazonica*, which is smaller than—but often mistaken for—the Blue-fronted, *A. aestiva.* Both are proven breeders. Amazons can be very aggressive to their owners when breeding, and for this reason nest boxes should have inspection doors outside of the flight; otherwise you will most certainly be attacked—and carrying a bird net does not always intimidate a pair. The tamer the birds are, the more violent will be their attacks, as they will have lost their fear of their owners.

Other species that will be available will be the Spectacled (White-fronted), *A. albifrons;* the Yellow-lored, *A. xantholora;* the Tucuman, *A. tucumana;* the Salvin's, *A. autumnalis salvini;* the Yellow-fronted (or one of its numerous subspecies), *A. ochrocephala,* and the Mealy, *A. farinosa.* Blue-fronts and Yellow-lores, the latter in particular, will be expensive. All Amazons are mainly green birds, but the exception is the endangered St. Vincent Amazon, *A. guildingii,* which is often various shades of yellow-orange-brown and gold and is a very striking bird.

Other South American Parrots

The parrots under this heading consist of some 22 species in eight genera, but only a few of them are regularly available in aviculture. The genus *Pionites* contains just two species, commonly known as

caiques, and these are the Black-headed, *P. melanocephala,* and the White-bellied, or White-breasted, Caique, *P. leucogaster.* Both species in fact have white breasts and abdomens but are easily distinguished. The first named has a black head, black beak, and grayish feet, while the White-bellied has the yellow feathers of the neck extending right over the head, with an ivory-colored beak and pink feet.

Caiques are interesting birds and can become extremely affectionate. On the negative side, they are very destructive, so aviaries will need to have the woodwork protected. They should be given a diet which includes plenty of fresh fruit and in general be regarded as though they were conures. They seem to be exceedingly social birds with their own kind and ideally should always be kept in pairs, this being especially true for aviary birds.

Pionus comprises eight

Nanday Conure. Under the right conditions, these birds can be regular and consistent breeders and are known for their good parenting abilities.

A Peach-faced Lovebird. Despite the fact that it can be quarrelsome toward other birds, the Peach-faced is still one of the more popular species of lovebirds.

Afro-Asian Parrots
THE AFRICAN GREY.

Unrivaled among parrots as a talking bird, the African Grey, *Psittacus erithacus*, is the only member of its genus. Three subspecies are recognized, though many authorities believe that *P. e. princeps* is not separable from the nominate race. Greys are not especially attractive birds, but they make up for this with their outstanding intelligence and powers of mimicry. On the negative side, they will feather-pluck themselves if not given considerable attention, and rarely display their talking prowess while strangers are present. When purchasing Greys, those sold as "silvers" are held to be the better talkers than the darker-colored birds of the *timneh* subspecies; this will be reflected in the asking price, which will be significantly lower in the latter case. Greys have been bred many times and require a deep nest box which should be left in place throughout the year. It is worth noting that beginners are apt to want things to happen quickly when they decide to become breeders of birds; when they do not, they start changing diets, nest boxes, and even aviaries. With many of the larger parrots—and indeed any non-

species of which the most usually available are the Blue-headed, *P. menstruus;* the Slaty-headed, *P. maximiliani;* and the Dusky, *P. fuscus.* The last species, though not vividly colored, will be the more expensive of these three parrots. The eminent parrot authority Rosemary Low considers the Blue-headed to be a far better choice as a pet bird for the average home than the Amazons. They are less noisy, less excitable and their bite is less powerful—three very attractive reasons for owning them—and they are most appealing. In price, they will cost much the same as a Blue-fronted Amazon but will be seen in far fewer stores or dealer lists. Each of these parrots will be between 24–28cm (9–11in) in length.

established strains of birds—the pairs must be given time; this can vary from a year to many years, so it is another reason to commence with very popular, established species rather than birds such as Greys.

THE GENUS *POICEPHALUS*. This genus contains nine species, including one or two which are

LOVEBIRDS. These delightful and very popular little birds, which range from 13–16.5cm (5–6.5in), are all members of the genus *Agapornis*, which contains nine species. All are available, with the exception of Swindern's, *A. swinderniana*, which is also known as the Black-collared. This species is unknown to

very popular pet and aviary birds, and are quite reasonable in price. The Senegal, *P. senegalus*, is the best known of the group and makes an excellent pet if acquired as a youngster.

aviculture. Of the others, the most popular are the Peach-faced, *A. roseicollis*; the Fischer's, *A. fischeri*; and the Masked, *A. personata*. The first two named are quite reasonably priced, but others, and

especially the many color-mutational forms, will be progressively more expensive depending on the species or color.

In an aviary, lovebirds will

quite happily coexist with other birds, but care should be exercised as all species of these little birds can be very aggressive. These are tough little critters and need to be with birds somewhat larger than themselves. They can be colony bred, but much fighting will ensue, so the novice is better advised to keep them as pairs. Peach-faced Lovebirds are especially prolific, and aggressive, and have the largest number of color forms (only the budgerigar has more). They can be bred in cages and will breed throughout the year. Budgerigar nest boxes will be fine. The species mentioned are not sexually dimorphic,

so buy only guaranteed true pairs. As pets they can be very amusing, and all in all make excellent birds for beginners.

RINGNECK PARAKEETS. This group of parrots consists of 13 species in the single genus *Psittacula*. Their center of distribution is the Indian subcontinent, but one species, the Rose-ringed Parakeet, is also found in Africa, thus giving this parrot the largest area of distribution of any member of the order Psittaciformes. They are a very popular group of birds in aviculture, and the Indian Ringneck (Rose-ringed), *P. krameri manillensis*, is by far the most numerous and least expensive. The African form, *P. k. krameri*, is very similar but usually a little more costly. Considering just how many millions have been exported over the years, the number bred in captivity is relatively small. This serves to illustrate that when species are allowed out of a country in vast numbers, therefore being very low-priced, breeders simply do not attempt to breed them. The economic factor has always been a prime consideration with the average aviculturist.

The ringnecks

Amazon parrots, in general, are predominantly green in their coloration. What can vary greatly is the coloration and patterning of their heads. Pictured: Orange-winged Amazons.

and Plum-heads, will happily live in a mixed aviary and rarely (in my own experience) bother other birds. Even the Alexandrine is a placid bird in mixed company, but its formidable beak should not be taken lightly, so one needs to know the individual bird's temperament before casually adding it to aviaries of mixed collections. At breeding times pairs are best housed on their own, though they can be colony bred; I well recall the magnificent sight of Indian Ringnecks kept

range in size from the Layard's (Emerald-collared), *P. calthorpe*, at 29cm (11in) to the Alexandrine, *P. eupatria*, at 58cm (22in). Half of the length is composed of the long tail feathers. There are lutino and blue mutations found in the Rose-ringed and the Alexandrine, and these are quite magnificent if expensive. Other mutations are found in the Indian Ringneck but those cited are the most attractive. The prettiest of the group is possibly the Plum-headed, *P. cyanocephala*, yet in its own way the Malabar Bluewing, *P. columboides*, with its subtle shades of green, is also very pleasing. In fact, the author is very fond of this whole group, and many consider the Derbyan, *P. derbiana*, to be one of the most attractive of all parakeets.

Ringnecks, especially Indians

in the enormous mixed aviary at Jerong park, Singapore. Here, they roost in the cliff sides of a waterfall which they swoop in and out of. A large aviary is best for all members of this group, and the singular reason that many species of birds cannot be kept in mixed collections is actually one of space limitations of the average bird keeper.

As pets, ringnecks make good companions, but few will allow you to touch them bodily. The larger species can be noisy at times, though their call is more pleasant than, say, those of conures or amazons. They must be given a large cage and they *must* be given plenty of time out of their cage. They are more nervous than the short-tailed parrots and need gentle and considerable patience to train. The large ones can be very destructive (to the woodwork) in aviaries, but I have experienced little of this problem with those I have kept as pets in a house, possibly because I ensure they have ample blocks of wood to keep them busy on their playforms. Of all the many parrots available to breeders, those of *Psittacula* I believe to represent both the best value for money and offering much scope for the future. The numerous mutations seen in the various species, together with the comparative rarity of others, is such that I am sure one day those who take the trouble to establish them will find it has proved to be a very worthwhile undertaking.

Pacific Parrots—The Cockatiel

This delightful little bird is like a miniature cockatoo, especially in its lutino (white) mutational form. It has the scientific name of *Nymphicus hollandicus* and is 32cm (12.5in) in length. I have kept many parrots over the years but would still rate this as the one which I would recommend as *the* ideal bird for a novice owner. It would be difficult, almost impossible, to

fault it. Acquired as babies, they tame very easily; they are large enough to not look delicate; they are very quiet, having a pleasant whistle; they are hardy, easy to breed, undemanding in their diet, and can be mixed with the smallest of finches with no fears at all of their bullying them (sometimes the reverse can be true!). They can be bred in cages, and there are numerous color mutations (but all based on gray, white, brown). If this were not enough, they are extremely modestly priced in their normal (wild) color, and will usually live for twenty years or more. The cock is somewhat more colorful than the hen, but both sexes have the same happy little character. I do not think I have met an aviculturist who has not, at some point, owned a

A Blue-headed Parrot, *Pionus menstruus*. This pretty parrot is distinguished by the violet-blue coloring on its head, neck, and breast. Fanciers of this species claim that it makes a very affectionate pet.

While it may not win raves in the beauty department, the African Grey possesses other desirable qualities. It is an intelligent bird, known for its great ability to talk.

Polytelis alexandrae, also known as the Princess of Wales, or Alexandra, Parakeet.

Cockatiel, nor have I ever heard a criticism of them.

Australian Parakeets

If it is color you like in an aviary, then the Australian parakeets will not be bettered. They are the most well-established of all parrots in captivity, come in a range of sizes and prices, and a number of them have various color mutations. They are generally hardy and uncomplicated in their dietary needs. On the negative side, a number of the larger species can be very aggressive and are not recommended to the beginner for mixed aviaries. In their homeland they are not referred to as "parakeets" but as "parrots." In all, there are 40 species in twelve genera, and of these possibly 35 are generally available to bird keepers. They are not suited to cage life, though certain of the smaller species have been kept as pets and I am advised they made fine companions. Of course, the world's number one pet is a parakeet: the ever-popular budgerigar; but it is so well known that it need not be included in this short review of the species.

Among the most popular of the small grass parakeets is the Bourke's, *Neophema bourkii*, a somewhat plainly colored bird 20cm (8in) in length. However, what it lacks in color it makes up for in being a quiet, peace-loving and very reliable breeder. It can be safely housed with other birds, even finches, and

A Tucuman Amazon, *Amazona tucumana.*

only when breeding should it be housed on its own, as the cocks can be aggressive at this time, though not always to other non-parrots. Bourke's are the least expensive of the grass parakeets, but the mutational colors—yellow, rose, and cinnamon—will cost substantially more.

In the same genus is the Splendid, or Scarlet-chested, *N. splendida*, a truly beautiful bird of 19cm (8in). It will cost more than the previous species, but its green, scarlet, yellow, and blue feathers always command attention from those seeing them for the first time. By nature they are very quiet and have a pleasant voice; they are well established in aviculture and cope with European and North American climates, providing they are not subject to damp conditions. The female lacks the scarlet chest, and the blue on the head is much reduced. Similar is the Turquoisine, *N. pulchella*, which lacks the scarlet chest; but it is presently cheaper in price and is very good

value. Even less colorful is the Elegant, *N. elegans*, but it is still most attractive and is gaining in popularity.

Somewhat larger parrots are found in the genus *Psephotus*, with the most popular being the Red-rump, *P. haematonotus*, with a length of 27cm (10.5in). This species is inexpensive, but the yellow mutation will be pricey. Red-rumps and others of this genus are very aggressive towards other parrotlike birds, including those much larger than themselves; however, they tend to ignore non-parrots. They are prolific breeders and also become very tame—but not in the cage-bird sense, a situation to which they are unsuited. Less available is the very pretty Many-colored Parakeet, *P. varius*, similar in size to the Red-rump. It is a reliable breeder.

A Fischer's Lovebird, *Agapornis fischeri.*

A Spectacled, or White-fronted, Amazon, *Amazona albifrons*. Spectacled Amazons do not thrive in a cage. It is better to house them in an aviary or birdroom.

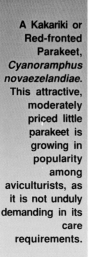

A Kakariki or Red-fronted Parakeet, *Cyanoramphus novaezelandiae*. This attractive, moderately priced little parakeet is growing in popularity among aviculturists, as it is not unduly demanding in its care requirements.

Of the other Australian parakeets, the Princess of Wales, or Alexandra, Parakeet, *Polytelis alexandrae*, can also make a suitable pet. This species has soft pastel shades of green, yellow, pink, and blue in its feathers, and this is very attractive; the drawback is that they can be rather noisy. They are one of the few Australian parakeets that can be colony bred. Another sociable member of this genus is the Barraband, or Superb, *P. swainsonii*, a bird of green with yellow forehead and throat, contrasting with a red upper breast. These are becoming quite popular, and this is reflected in their relatively modest price.

The last parakeet to be discussed here is the Kakariki of New Zealand, *Cyanoramphus novaezelandiae*. This fine little parrot of 28cm (11in) is a relative newcomer to aviculture but has proved so prolific that its price is very low. It is a green bird with red forehead and gray-white beak. Its numbers in the wild were so low that reintroduction from captive-bred birds was undertaken— and very successfully too. It is quiet and breeds when very young, so has much to recommend it.

A lovely pied Orange-fronted Conure.

Index